This Notebook Belongs To

_____

A GARDENER'S NOTEBOOK

LIFE WITH MY GARDEN

DOUG OSTER AND JESSICA WALLISER

st. lynn's
press

PITTSBURGH

A Gardener's Notebook
Life With My Garden

Copyright 2011 © Doug Oster and Jessica Walliser

ISBN-13: 978-0-9819615-7-6

Second Edition, 2011

First Edition, 2008, titled A Gardener's Journal
ISBN-13: 978-0-976761-7-8

St. Lynn's Press . POB 18680 . Pittsburgh, PA 15236
412.466.0790 • www.stlynnspress.com

Typesetting–Holly Rosborough, Network Printing Services
Cover Design–Heidi Spurgin
Editor–Catherine Dees

Printed in Singapore by Tien Wah Press

This title and all of St. Lynn's Press books may be purchased for educational, business, or sales promotional use. For information please write:
Special Markets Department . St. Lynn's Press . POB 18680 . Pittsburgh, PA 15236

10 9 8 7 6 5 4 3 2 1

To Our Fellow Gardeners

A garden notebook can be as valuable to you as a good shovel or a favorite hoe. It's a place to record not only the gardener's daily chores, but successes and failures, lessons and losses. More than a record of the date of the last frost or when the first ripe tomato was picked, this notebook is meant to be a sort of diary for the garden, chronicling both the tangible events and the internal sentiments of the gardening day. If you're like most gardeners, your life is intertwined with the life of your garden. Simply jotting down what you did today and your feelings as you did it, not only preserves practical information, but creates a personal history of the resident gardener.

So many of us were inspired to garden by our parents and grandparents. What a gift it would be if we could know why they selected their plants and what was on their minds as they worked – the small moments that connect us to one another across time. This notebook is meant to live on as a family heirloom, to record the evolution of the family as well as the garden. We have both enjoyed many winter days reading back through our old garden journals, watching the kids and sunflowers grow all over again. There is a lot of joy in reading what excited us about our gardens – spring entries filled with unmatched enthusiasm, and entries at the end of the season conveying a feeling of relief that the gardening months are at an end.

We don't want to give the impression that you'll need to write something every day (though looking back on old notebooks will always bring wishes for more entries). Whenever you can steal a few spare moments, take pen to paper and record what comes to mind – whether it's expressing frustration over a lost trowel, or conveying the excitement of digging potatoes with the grandkids.

When we were writing our recent book, *Grow Organic,* we envisioned one day creating this personal notebook for our gardening friends to enjoy. It's our hope that this notebook can become a legacy for your family – a way to remember not only the passion you felt for gardening, but those small, intimate moments that make life in the garden so meaningful.

Warm regards,
Jess and Doug

P.S. Because we're gardeners ourselves, we couldn't help passing on to you some of our favorite tips and personal garden memories. You'll find them tucked here and there on these pages, along with a seed-planting guide for your veggies and an easy how-to for composting.

P.P.S. You'll also notice that we've included graphed pages at the end of the notebook so you can create, and play with, designs for your garden. We recommend using an erasable pencil!

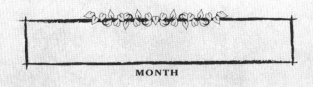

MONTH

MULCH RING

Give your trees a bit of
a buffer. Surround the
trunks with a wide ring
of mulch (making sure it
doesn't touch the trunk
itself). This "moat" will
serve as protection from
the lawn mower and
string trimmer. And it
will allow you to easily
examine the bark for
signs of borers and
other damage.

FOR THE BIRDS

Protect blueberries, strawberries and other small fruits from birds by covering the plants with bird netting. You can build a frame from PVC pipe or untreated lumber, cover it with netting and place it over the plants. Make the frame portable so you can use it only until the harvest is complete.

VINE BORER PREVENTION

To prevent squash vine borers from attacking the base of your zucchini and squash plants, cut a strip of aluminum foil about 2 inches by 6 inches, and wrap it loosely around the stem. Do this as close to the soil as possible and the adult insect won't land there to lay its eggs.

LIVING MULCH

❧

Using cover crops as living mulch is an awesome labor saver. Plant red clover, alfalfa or another green manure right underneath your squash, pumpkins, peppers, tomatoes and cucumbers. No weeds will compete with the cover crop and you'll cut down on your watering by having less soil exposed to evaporation.

DRAGONFLIES

If you have a pond or wetlands in your garden you probably already have dragonflies. Create a buffer zone of 3 to 4 feet around your pond by allowing wildflowers and bog plants to grow un-mown. This will provide habitat and marginal areas for dragon and damsel flies to perch and lay their eggs. They eat huge numbers of mosquitoes and other flying garden pests.

'MATERS

To save tomato seeds, pick a ripe fruit and squeeze out some of the seeds with their accompanying slime. Let the seeds soak overnight in a glass of water then drain, rinse and add new water. Do this for 3 days in a row to allow the slime to ferment off. Then spread the seeds on a paper towel to dry. After a week, pack them into envelopes, label them and put them in an airtight container in the fridge.

the garden dog

Her name was Pearl and she was truly a garden dog. In her prime she was an uncatchable Australian sheep dog, fleet of foot, who would run circles around me as I chased her around the neighborhood. I first recognized her love of garden produce on a lazy afternoon after I'd picked some kale. As I stood there, kale in hand talking to my wife, I heard a crunching noise and felt tugging on the recently severed stalks. Pearl was eating kale?

That summer was my first for growing heirloom tomatoes. Johnny's Selected Seeds had sent me 'Pruden's Purple,' and I anxiously waited for the heritage tomatoes to ripen. In August the first tomato began a pink blush that had my mouth watering. Then its color deepened to a dark red, on its way to purple. One afternoon I looked out the bathroom window to see Pearl pulling off my prize tomato. I screamed as I lit out of the house sprinting towards the garden. She looked up, faked left and took off around the yard. After a short chase I rescued my half-eaten prize.

My wife and I laughed about it that night and I wrote a column about it for the newspaper I worked for at the time. The day after the story ran I stood in court covering a trial. During a break, the judge looked down at me from the bench and asked, "You ate the other half of that tomato didn't you?" And I told the truth. "Yes your honor, I ate the tomato." The judge and bailiff couldn't stifle their laughter and neither could I.

Pearl passed away this year, but I'll always remember her as the young dog who kept me running and who loved veggies from the garden as much as I do.

Doug

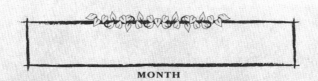

MONTH

KEEP THE BERRIES COMIN'

Most varieties of red raspberries produce two annual crops. To get the most from your raspberry patch, prune them properly. In early spring, cut any canes that have already fruited (you'll see the old berry cluster) clear to the ground. For the canes that haven't yet fruited, cut them back only to the uppermost green bud – these canes will provide the summer crop. Any new canes emerging from the ground will provide the autumn harvest.

TULIPS FOREVER

Many gardeners are surprised to hear that most hybrid tulips are meant to give only one year's bloom. For truly perennial tulips that return bigger and better every season, plant Darwin or Gregii tulips. Most quality bulb catalogs will categorize tulips by their type and these are the two to look for.

KITTIES GONE WILD

To keep feral and neighborhood cats out of the garden, try using a natural scent repellant around the garden's perimeter. Motion activated sprinklers are also quite successful. When these sprinklers sense an intruder entering the area they send out a quick burst of water, scaring the cat (or deer or dog) away and deterring their return.

WARM TOOTSIES

Keep fingers and toes
toasty while performing
late autumn and
winter garden chores
by purchasing battery
powered socks and
gloves. Good quality
ones are shock resistant
even when wet and
are easy to wash
and maintain.

OF LEAVES
AND PONDS

A week or so before
autumn leaf drop, spread
plastic mesh bird netting
over the pond to keep out
falling foliage. Secure
the edges with rocks or
bricks, being sure the
netting doesn't contact
the water surface. This
simple practice keeps the
pond free of debris and
makes spring cleaning
much easier.

HEAVING PERENNIALS

During winter's
freeze-thaw cycles,
newly planted perennials
may "heave" out of the
soil. Walk through the
garden often during the
winter months and simply
step down any plants
whose root balls have
popped out of the soil.
Doing this frequently
will help prevent
winter damage to
any exposed roots.

about a new beginning

With a young toddler, career changes, and commute distance in mind, my husband and I found it necessary to sell our farm and move closer to the city. I was heartbroken to leave my enormous "garden," and going from 25 acres to two has presented me with some tough decisions. I went from growing food and flowers for hundreds of farmers market customers to growing only for the three of us. The biggest difficulty has been deciding how to pare down my selections; now I have to plant only what I really love and I definitely have less room to experiment. This, as it turns out, has not been a bad thing.

Since downsizing, I have found myself paying closer attention to all the details that had fallen neglected on the farm. For the first time in years, I have a weed-free garden; and instead of looking only at the big production picture, I'm now able to focus on creating the intimate, personal garden areas I've always wanted. I can now appreciate plants for their individual beauty and am enjoying building beautiful combinations of container plantings and festive veggies. Don't get me wrong, there's still lots of work to be done to make the garden "mine," but I feel this garden growing on me, and I love it more every day.

My son, too, is thriving in this new garden. Feeding him home-grown blueberries right off the branches, watching him try to find the fish swimming in our small pond, and seeing him absolutely filthy with earth makes it crystal clear that it doesn't matter how much you grow, just that you do. Growing a child and a garden side-by-side has brought me overwhelming peace and happiness. I hope more parents give it a try.

Jess

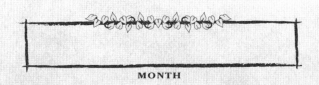

MONTH

No More Algae

To keep ponds and other garden water features free of string algae, place a small bale of barley straw in the water before the algae takes hold. These bales are widely available at pet and aquatic stores and are much less expensive than their chemical counterparts. The decomposition of the dried barley releases compounds that help deter the growth of algae.

BLIND PEONIES

When planting peonies, keep the roots only about an inch below the soil surface. Any deeper and you'll have a blind peony (the "eyes" won't produce flowers).

LATE BLOOMERS

If the end of the growing season is lackluster in your perennial border, try planting a few late blooming varieties. Monkshood, dwarf plumbago, Japanese anemone, asters, toadlilies and turtlehead are just a few of the many plants that produce lovely autumn flowers. And don't forget about the ornamental grasses – their foliage and flower fronds are beautiful additions to the fall and winter landscape.

SOWING HERB SEEDS

Many common non-hardy herbs are easy to start from seed directly in the garden. Toss down seeds of cilantro, chervil, calendula, chamomile, borage, sweet marjoram and coriander after the danger of frost has passed. An added bonus: most of these varieties will readily self-sow, saving you the effort of planting new seeds in subsequent seasons.

EXTENDING THE VASE LIFE

To keep cut flowers beautiful longer, add a few drops of household bleach to the vase of water. The bleach will cut down on stem-clogging bacteria. Empty, wash and refill the vase as often as possible and re-cut the stems every few days.

GOING UNDERGROUND

Underground veggies
– like beets, turnips,
rutabagas, radish, carrots
and horseradish – use a
lot of phosphorus.
Since this essential
nutrient is only
available in a small
zone surrounding the
plant's roots, be sure to
side-dress rows of these
crops with an organic
fertilizer slightly higher in
phosphorus. Bonemeal
is a great choice.

in appreciation of simple plants

There are two plants that will always hold a special place in my heart. They aren't fancy; anyone can grow them with ease, but they are a link to my past.

The first are early blooming yellow crocus. These were one of the things that bloomed right outside our front door. I can remember getting the mail on the way home from school and running up our driveway to be greeted by these cheery blooms that only lasted a few days. For some reason they just resonated with me, the luminescent color, the fragility of the petals and the fact that my mother – even though she wasn't much of a gardener – had planted them years before.

Every year around Memorial Day weekend, there was always a new flat of marigolds planted around the foundation of our modest 1950's ranch. I used to spend the long summer days lying prostrate on the white clover that was in the grass, to get a close look at the intricate colors; reds, yellows and oranges intertwined together in the most fascinating ways.

And the scent was intoxicating. I wouldn't have used that exact word when I was a boy, but that's what it was. Most people don't like the aroma of marigolds but for me it instantly transports me back to those endless days of running barefoot through rows of pure white hanging sheets that filled the suburban backyards.

Doug

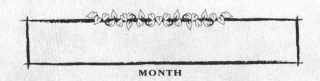

MONTH

SELF-PLANTING PLANTS

What could be easier
than a garden that plants
itself? Many beautiful
non-hybridized varieties
of annuals will readily
self-sow each year,
making a seasonal
return performance
a surefire bet.
Favorite self-sowing
varieties include
snow-on-the-mountain,
cosmos, ageratum,
larkspur, catchfly,
forget-me-nots,
love-in-a-mist,
sunflower, salvia and
flowering tobacco.

CISTERNS

Commonly found on old
farms and homesteads,
cisterns are increasingly
popular in suburban
America, as gardeners
begin to realize the
importance of using
harvested rainwater
to irrigate their crops.
These underground
plastic water storage
tanks are located beneath
the frost line and capture
rain from downspouts for
later use. Cisterns are
relatively inexpensive to
buy and install, giving
you plenty of free water
for the garden and
helping our over-taxed,
outdated storm sewers
manage excess rainfall.

CLEAN AND GLEAN

At season's end, collect any fallen fruit from the orchard floor and pluck any remaining diseased fruit from the branches.

This simple cultural practice aids in deterring over-wintering pests and fungal spores, simplifying organic control of both issues the following year.

DIVIDE AND CONQUER

Late summer is the best time to divide German bearded iris – and to battle the iris borer. Dig up the iris clump and crack apart the rhizomes. Should you see any smelly, rotten root sections, you will likely find a few borers (fat, pink grub-like larvae). Squash the borers then replant the divided rhizomes so the top half of the root sits above the soil surface. Then cut the foliage back halfway. Be sure to angle the cut so water doesn't sit on the blunt end, causing rot or other bacterial problems.

Manure Safety

Animal manures may contain E. coli or other dangerous pathogens, so using them properly is a must. Be sure to fully compost them with other ingredients in the compost bin, or apply well-aged manure to veggie gardens a minimum of 120 days before harvest. Your compost pile must reach 160 degrees for at least 15 days in a row in order to kill the pathogens. Turning it regularly will assure that the temperature gets nice and hot.

LEVEL DEADHEADING

Removing spent flowers is
a necessity in the summer
garden. It will keep your
plants looking fresh and
blooming continually.
If you aren't sure how
far back to make a
deadheading cut, simply
follow the flower stem
back to its uppermost
leaf and make the cut
just above it. Though
certain plants prefer to
be cut back further, this
technique is usually
a safe bet.

about memorial seeds

My Nana grew up on the farm that belonged to her parents, grandparents, and great grandparents. Since 1748, this lovely property in eastern Pennsylvania has been home to our ancestors. My great-uncle Paul and his wife Miriam (two of the sweetest folks you'll ever meet) still live there, despite being well into their 80's, and with various health concerns.

Nana loved the farm and the quiet little valley it nestles in. It was there that she learned much of her passion for growing, and – from her mother and father – her ability to work hard with little complaint. When she passed away several years ago, my sister and I wanted to share a piece of the farm and her love of gardening with family and friends. Before the memorial service, which was held under a tent in Nana's back garden, we collected seeds from her snow-on-the-mountain and larkspur. I remember being very touched when she explained to me a few years prior that she had grown these plants from seeds she'd collected long ago at the farm, along with the divisions she'd made of lily of the valley, daylilies, and ferns. During the eulogy, we passed around a notebook asking guests who were interested in growing these family heirlooms to provide us with a mailing address.

Over the next week, I mailed 32 packets of seeds. I included cultural instructions for growing the plants and one of my Nana's favorite poems. It was wonderful, healing therapy for me and I felt like, in some small way, I was helping my Nana's garden live on.

Jess

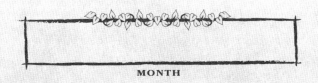

MONTH

ENDOPHYTE-ENHANCED GRASS

Some varieties of turf grass seed now come "innoculated" with a naturally occurring fungus. This fungus enhances the plant's immunity to disease and hardiness, and helps it produce compounds that ward off pests. However, very few studies have been done regarding any possible effects on pets who consume the grass plants. Also, you should not use endophyte-enhanced grass where livestock will graze, as it does not make good forage.

PRUNE BY BLOOM

Some woody shrubs
flower on old wood,
while others do so on
new growth, so pruning
at the wrong time could
mean the removal of
future flowers. A general
rule of thumb: a bloom
time prior to June 15th
occurs on old wood, while
flowers after June 15th
appear on new growth.
Early bloomers
(old-wood) should be
pruned immediately after
bloom. Shrubs whose
flowers appear on new
wood should be trimmed
in fall, winter or very
early spring.

GRUBS

To control Japanese beetle larvae feeding on the roots of turf grass and ornamentals, don't water your lawn during the summer months. Newly laid eggs and recently hatched larvae need moisture to survive, so allowing your grass to go dormant in the summer helps keep their population in check. In spring, turn over a square foot of sod. If you find 10 or more grubs, treat the entire lawn with the natural biological insecticide called milky spore. If used according to manufacturer's directions, milky spore can remain effective for 15 years!

PLANTING A TREE

One of the most common
causes of tree death
is improper planting.
Planting too deeply or
too shallowly will indeed
kill a tree, though it can
take several years. Also,
adding amendments to
the backfill soil during
planting encourages root
circling and may lead to
girdling and death. Our
recommended method: for
balled and burlapped trees,
dig the hole twice as wide
as, but no deeper than, the
attached root ball. Without
"breaking" the root ball,
place the tree in the hole,
cut off the wire cage with
pliers, remove all twine and
nails, cut off the top half
of the burlap, and backfill
the hole with the same soil
that came out of it. Water
regularly through the
first full year.

SUNFLOWERS AND GRASS

❧

If you put a bird feeder in your lawn and fill it with sunflowers, the grass beneath it will eventually die. The seed coats of sunflowers contain a compound that prevents other plants from growing (its called allelopathy), so to prevent a bare spot in the lawn be sure to move the feeder every week or two.

Moss

The presence of moss in your lawn may indicate a fertility or pH problem. Get your soil tested to know for sure. If it's in a shady area, be sure to re-seed with a mix heavy in fescue; it thrives in shadier conditions. We don't necessarily think moss is a bad thing — at least it's green!

a place to sit

Sometimes it's hard on my kids to have a dad like me, especially on trash days when we're out in my pick-up and I'm driving slowly along the curb. They know the drill – Dad's looking for stuff. When I eye an old garden bench or an Adirondack chair, I can't bear to see it sent to a landfill.

I think every garden should have plenty of places to sit. I've filled mine with curbside treasures. When I take a break from garden work, a new world presents itself to my eyes, because only when we stop do we really see the beauty of the tiny details that have escaped us. For me it happens when I sit on the bench I set along a trail through our woods – and I can observe the soft green moss that under inspection reveals wonderful textures and tiny brow seed heads. With a place to sit, what once was invisible becomes something to be enjoyed and studied.

A rescued 1950's wooden lawn chair in another part of the garden offers me views of a tall scraggly pine tree painted amber by the late afternoon sun. Just a few feet from a birdfeeder, it also provides close-up views and sounds of songbirds as they soar in and out, enjoying copious amounts of the black oil sunflower seeds that keep them plump and healthy.

So the next time you drive by some old garden furniture earmarked for the landfill, stop and throw it in the car, then find a place for it in the garden for what will be the best seat in the house.

Doug

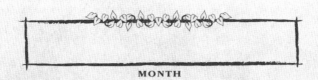

MONTH

NIGHT TIME IS THE RIGHT TIME

❧

If you've got a day job and the only time you get to enjoy your garden is at dusk, plant an evening garden. These gardens are filled with plants that exhibit nighttime fragrance and often have white, luminescent blooms. Locate the evening garden very near your outdoor living space so you can spend time enjoying the garden during dinner and a glass of wine. Plants that shine in the evening garden include Datura, moonflower, Nicotiana, Heliotrope, sweet alyssum and Brugmansia.

SALTY

Salt damage from roads, sidewalks and driveways can wreak havoc on both your soil and your plants. Gardens adjacent to salted areas should be planted with salt tolerant varieties like Clethra, inkberry and Japanese holly, bayberry and beautyberry.

THE BEES HAVE IT

❧

Plant a garden filled with flowers that will attract native bees in addition to European honeybees. Leafcutter, bumble, sweat and digger bees are just a few of our native species. Try growing tickseed, bee balm and goldenrod near crops that you'd like to pollinate. These native bees don't travel far from their nests, so planting nectar sources close to vegetables is a terrific way to lure them in.

INVASION

One way to simplify your life in the garden is to pay attention to the potential invasiveness of any plants you are introducing. If a catalog touts a plant as quick spreading, watch out. Some species can quickly outgrow their desired location and crowd out more desirable plants. Your county's co-operative extension agency can also provide you with a list of invasive species in your area.

MILDEW PREVENTION

Mix 1 tablespoon of baking soda and ½ teaspoon of mild dish soap with a half-gallon of water to make an organic fungicide that will help prevent black spot and powdery mildew. Begin to spray early in the season and continue every 2 or 3 weeks.

SIMPLE STRAWBERRIES

❧

Plant bare root strawberries in early spring and remove any flowers they produce for the first year. This allows them to establish a good root system and to increase production in following years. The most common problem with strawberries is botrytis, a fungal disease that turns the ripening fruit into a ball of fuzzy mush. There isn't much you can do about it except make sure your strawberries have plenty of room to grow, mulch with straw between the plants to keep the berries off the ground, and hope for drier conditions.

about playing in the rain

When I was growing up in our middle class neighborhood, every child around hit the streets after summer thunderstorms and during warm afternoon rain showers, ready to play in the huge puddles that formed at the street intersections. There was no greater pleasure than making instant mud pies and meatballs as the raindrops fell to the ground. No one wore raincoats and my mother never seemed to care that I had to strip off my wet, muddy clothes on the porch before coming inside. Splashing in the puddles, racing tiny sailboats made of leaves and toothpicks down the gutters, feeling how quickly the hot asphalt cooled – those were some of the activities that made summer, summer.

These days, I see fancy rain slickers and galoshes and multi-colored umbrellas in kids' clothing stores, but I never see anyone out playing in them. At most, I'll see kids dashing for the bus, or running from the car into the store as fast as they can, all decked out in fancy rain garb, their mothers telling them to get a move-on before they get wet.

Rain is the best water source for gardens, and it's the most underappreciated "toy" out there – for kids and adults alike. Though it may not be as pure as it used to be, rain contains no chlorine and very few dissolved minerals. It's naturally purified through the Earth's living filtration system of plants and soil; and as long as rain continues to fall, transpiring plants and evaporation will continue to power the water cycle. Promise me that during the next warm summer shower you'll go outside barefoot, turn your face skyward and play.

Jess

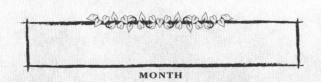

MONTH

SMART PLANT PICKS

One of the easiest ways to reduce the amount of chemicals needed in your garden is to choose pest resistant varieties. When shopping for new plants, do a little research. Find out which choices aren't prone to diseases like powdery mildew or bacterial wilt. Ask gardening friends which plants are most resilient in their gardens.

WEEDS

If weeds are the pest you are looking to prevent, try corn gluten meal. It's a by-product of the processing of corn and acts as a pre-emergent herbicide: it prevents seeds from sprouting. Use it on the lawn and in the perennial border. Just be sure not to use it where you'll be growing plants from seed. With regular use, it can prevent 90% of weed seeds from germinating. Imagine 90% less weeds to pull!

WATER

Make sure your plants are never left high and dry. Most garden plants need 1 inch of water per week to thrive. If you let your plants get too dry, they will suffer from "water stress." The biggest symptom, of course, is wilting; but regularly subjecting your plants to this stress will reduce their natural immunity, causing them to be more susceptible to problems.

THE SNIFF TEST

When buying
commercially produced
compost either in bags
or bulk, ask to smell it.
No reputable nursery
will turn you down. It
should smell earthy and
musty, not acidic or sour.
Always ask if the compost
was made using sewage
sludge – an ingredient,
in our opinions, not
considered safe for
organic gardens.

LACEWING LARVAE

These immature insects look a lot like ladybug larvae, except they are light brown with pale markings around their margins. They also have large, curved mandibles. Their favorite foods include aphids, mealybugs, mites and scale.

TRENCHING

If you don't have the
space for an official
compost bin, try the
burial method. Dig
trenches in the garden
and bury your kitchen
scraps and grass clippings
in them. By next season,
this material will have
decomposed and you
can plant your tomatoes
right on top of it.
You'll notice a
definite increase in
the earthworm
population too!

about a moment of truth

Many gardeners have an epiphany that leads them down the organic path. Mine happened after work one summer afternoon. I was new to gardening and relied mainly on the advice of conventional gardeners. When I started to see green caterpillars on my cabbage, I did what many novices do – I panicked. I called my friends and was told to dust the plants with Sevin. So I went down to the hardware store, bought a bag of the insecticide and covered the plants with the powder.

I stood triumphant as I looked over the garden, the conquering hero who had destroyed the invading force so determined to annihilate my crop.

As I stood there, smugly congratulating myself, my three-year-old son started to walk down the center path of the garden barefoot in search of some snow peas to pick off the vine.

My smugness turned to dread in the pit of my stomach, and I thought, "What have I done?" That was my awakening – the innocence of a little boy searching for a fresh treat.

It was the last day I ever used chemicals in the garden, and my first as an organic gardener. I reveled in the fact that I was going to learn how to grow without pesticides or herbicides and finally take control of my own garden.

It has been a wonderful journey of discovery and it's not over yet!

Doug

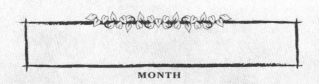

MONTH

Hornworm "Eggs"

When you find a
hornworm on your
'maters, carefully examine
it before removing it from
the plant. If you find
white, oval eggs hanging
off its back, the worm
has been parasitized by
wasps. It stops feeding
shortly after the eggs are
laid, so it's no longer a
threat to your tomatoes.
If you kill it, the eggs
will not hatch and your
garden will be robbed
of another generation of
these beneficial wasps.
Just leave the
hornworm alone.

Lady Larvae

Since ladybug larvae are heavy-duty aphid consumers, it's important to be able to identify them. They look like miniature alligators and are dark grey with red markings. Get to know them; they are about as beneficial as you can get!

TILLER VS. SHOVEL

If possible, use a shovel to turn the garden, not a tiller. Soil structure can be altered by excessive tilling. Digging the soil by hand is a great workout and a good way to examine the quality of soil in each bed.

DILL

For us, there is one plant that stands above all others for attracting beneficial insects: dill. It's one of the easiest plants to grow and once it's gone to seed your garden will always have the plants popping up each summer. Dill attracts a plethora of beneficial insects including parasitic wasps, hoverflies and lacewings; and it tastes pretty good with pickles too! The herb is also reported to repel aphids and spider mites. Some gardeners sprinkle it on the ground near squash plants to foil the squash bugs.

CAPABLE CLOVER

Allow white clover to grow in your lawn. Not only will it provide nitrogen to help keep your grass green, but it will draw tons of beneficial insects and pollinators to the yard.

CANNED BEES

You can buy orchard mason bees in a can. The cylinder contains both adult bees and nesting tubes and you simply hang it up in the garden. Docile mason bees are perfect pollinators for the orchard and veggie patch. They will not harm people and are native to most of the U.S.

about homegrown pleasures

Gardening on a half-acre suburban lot did not deter my mother. Back then, everyone in our neighborhood had a big garden to help feed their families. What everyone did not have was a backyard orchard. My parents planted a peach, nectarine, pear, apricot, plum, two cherry trees, an apple, three blueberry bushes, two grape vines, black raspberries, a strawberry patch and two filbert trees on that small lot.

I have great memories (and the pictures to back them up) of standing on ladders to harvest peaches as big as my head. All the neighbor kids would help with the picking; they knew they'd get to take some fruit home as payment. I remember my mom drying apple and nectarine slices in our food dehydrator and spreading out puréed fruits to make homemade fruit leather. And I remember my sister and me being disappointed each year there were no cherries (turns out we never did get any).

Some of my nicest garden memories involve my neighbor Rosie's grandchildren, Joel and Ryan. They hovered over the strawberry patch while we picked, ready and willing to share the fruit. In fact, my mom still calls them "stowberries" – the mispronounced name created by two little boys.

Summer harvests, of both fruit and fun, are unforgettable. Take time to teach your children and grandchildren about the delights of the garden. Dig for potatoes, collect berries in a metal colander, pick apples by flashlight…whatever you do, do it together.

Jess

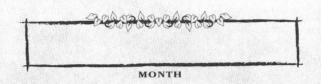

MONTH

SAVE THE LOVE

To save caladium, dahlia and canna tubers, dig them out after frost has blackened the foliage. Knock off the dirt, dry them for a day on newspaper then store them in a box of vermiculite or peat moss at around 50 degrees. Don't store them where temperatures will dip below freezing. Next spring, pot them up; or plant them directly in the garden after the last frost.

FOUR-SEASON SHRUBS

When shopping for shrubs, look for selections that will offer more than one season of interest to your landscape. Choose varieties that not only have beautiful flowers, but interesting bark or fall foliage. Shrubs with small fruits, like many viburnums or beautyberries, can add a lot of color to the winter garden. And when designing your perennial bed, plan on incorporating a few shrubs, both blooming and evergreen. They will provide winter interest, summer height and habitat for pest-eating birds.

HERE FISHY, FISHY

For an instant boost, especially for container plantings, try fish emulsion. It's a liquid fertilizer made from fish by-products. A great natural version of those blue chemical liquid fertilizers, fish emulsion will not burn foliage or stain hands.

THROW IN THE TOWEL

Knowing when to give up on a plant can be a challenge. If a favorite specimen (or an expensive one) isn't performing up to par, try a relocation, then give it two seasons to prove its worth. If it's finally time to throw in the towel, don't feel guilty about giving up; sometimes plants look great in the catalog or at the nursery, but they are too fussy for the garden.

SUCCESSION CUKES

Plant a second crop
of cucumbers a couple
of weeks after the first.
They will be planted off
the cycle of the cucumber
beetle and will be more
likely to survive.

SUCCESS WITH CORN

Plant corn in blocks, as
opposed to rows. The
plant is wind-pollinated;
more ears will be
produced if corn is sown
in blocks of at least
4 rows by 4 rows.

legacy of a tree

Rose of Sharon. Yes, I know it's a hated name to some gardeners, and it can overwhelm the yard with babies as it drops fertile seed everywhere – but it's the easiest of all trees to grow. It blooms in mid-summer in shades of white and purple, and the flowers last for weeks. There was a fine one in my old garden. That earlier garden had been the place where I began the long journey of discovery as a gardener, but more importantly, as a father.

My young children would play basketball next to that original tree; it withstood countless errant shots and diving saves, attempts to keep the ball in-bounds. When the kids stumbled into a yellow jacket nest, it was in the shadow of that tree that their mother and I dried their tears.

But then, with the prospect of another career, I moved away. I couldn't go without digging up one of my tree's offspring to take with me to my new garden. As I pulled out of the driveway for the final time – leaving the old garden after 15 wonderful years – the last thing I saw was my old Rose of Sharon.

I had a truckload of memories potted up in the bed for the long journey to their new home. And right on top was a young, four-foot tall Rose of Sharon, there for the memories and to keep a tradition going.

Doug

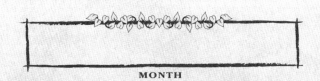

MONTH

CUTWORMS

To deter the dreaded
cutworm (these little
critters chop off stalks of
plants like a lumberjack),
put a toothpick on either
side of the stem of newly
planted seedlings. The
worm is unable to circle
the plant and is foiled.
Collars of toilet
paper tubes cut to
1-inch-high work too.

PICKING RIGHT

Always harvest your veggies in the morning. This is when their moisture content is at its highest and they will store longer. Instead of pulling, cut tomatoes, peppers, cukes and other fruits off the plants. That way you won't risk tearing the stem.

FEEDING WHILE WATERING – COMPOST TEA

Compost tea is a great supplemental fertilizer. Just put 5 or 6 shovelfuls of fresh, homemade compost in a burlap bag and steep it in a bucket of water until it's the color of strong tea. Use the finished product for watering.

ROW COVERS

This lightweight white fabric is made to float on top of plants and provide a barrier from feeding or breeding insects. It is very useful in the veggie patch and deters cabbage looper, flea beetles, squash vine borers, carrot maggots, squash bugs, berry-eating birds, aphids, grasshoppers, leaf hoppers and others. For crops where pollination is necessary, be sure to remove the fabric when the flowers open. Heavier weight fabrics can also be used as frost protection.

THE FINAL CUT

For your lawn, your last mow of the season should be about 1/2 inch shorter than usual. This helps prevent the grass blades from falling over and getting matted down under snow cover.

Winter Gardening

An early fall sowing of cool season greens like kale, collards, chard and lettuce can be harvested through most of the winter months – with a little extra protection. Make 18-inch-high semi-circles of heavy gage wire to form hoops over the rows. Cover this "tunnel" with heavyweight row cover or clear plastic sheeting. Weigh down the edges with soil or rocks and simply lift to harvest. Make sure to put your tunnels up before a hard frost to help capture heat and keep the soil temperatures warm. Heavily mulching the soil with straw, hay or grass clippings will help as well. There's nothing better than bragging to other gardeners about harvesting in January!

about a beech

A few years back, clients of mine had a beautiful young copper beech tree growing next to their perennial border. When the tree's upper branches began to be defoliated, the homeowner asked me to investigate. I found the culprit: tussock moth caterpillars. Knowing that the common biological control Bt would eliminate the problem, I made a single application.

Educating people about organic gardening also means teaching them patience. Bt stops the caterpillars from feeding immediately, but they don't actually die and fall off the plant until some time later. I explained this to the homeowners, assuring them that no more damage would be done to the tree.

Two days later, the landscaper came to mow the lawn and noticed the defoliation on the beech tree. He decided to take matters into his own hands and sprayed the tree with a very strong synthetic product. The day was over 90 degrees and the sun was out full force. Within a few days after the synthetic application the tree was completely defoliated; not a leaf remained. I asked the homeowners what happened, and after questioning the landscaper we had our answer. To top off the story, the landscaper then decided the tree was dead and cut it down, all the way to the ground!

Plants are resilient. They can handle a lot of damage, both from nature and man. You not only have to be patient with the remedy, but be patient with the plant. Let it have a season or two to rebound....*before* you break out the chainsaw.

Jess

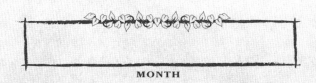

MONTH

GROUNDHOGS

You can't fence them out because they either climb over it or burrow under it. You've got a few choices: live trap them, eradicate them or get a low electric fence.

A single strand of electrified wire (solar powered ones are great) placed around the perimeter of the garden about 5 inches from ground level works great.

EARWIGS IN CARDBOARD

If you have earwig troubles in the garden, place a few pieces of corrugated cardboard around the infested plants. They like to shelter in the "tunnels" between layers. Each morning shake the cardboard into a plastic bag to chase out the hiding insects, then put the cardboard back in the garden.

BULBS WITH GRAVEL

Gophers, chipmunks and mice love to eat bulbs. When you plant them each fall, put a few handfuls of sharp gravel or crushed oyster shells in the hole first, then put in the bulbs. Top with a few more handfuls of gravel before covering over with soil. The pointed edges will keep them from digging through to the bulbs.

POISON IVY

Here's a great way to safely remove poison ivy plants. Wearing protective clothing and gloves, dig out as much of the base of the plant as you can (be sure to wash the shovel and handle afterwards). Put a garbage bag (or two) over your hand and up your arm. Pick up the plant tops then flip the bag inside-out over it – pretend you are picking up a pile of dog poop. Seal the bag and throw it away. Wash up promptly, using one of the poison ivy washes you can now find at your local pharmacy.

Ridding
Groundcover
of Grass

❧

When grass has found
its way into your
Pachysandra, myrtle,
winter creeper or other
groundcovers, try this
method. Let the grass
blades get fairly long,
but do not allow them
to flower. Put on a
chemical-resistant rubber
glove, then a cotton
glove on top of that.
Soak a rag or sponge
in an organic herbicide
and grasp the tops of
the grass with it. Pull
the rag and the cotton
glove along the length
of the grass, being
careful to avoid the
plants underneath. This
will kill the grass while
leaving the groundcover
unscathed.

BUTTERFLY LARVAE

When you encounter a caterpillar in the garden that you aren't familiar with, be sure to identify it before taking any action. It may be the larvae of any number of pollinating butterflies or moths. And be careful – some caterpillars, even beautiful ones, may have hairs that can give you a nasty sting.

about one heck of a bug

It was an amazing sight: a big scary-looking wasp, with what appeared to be a 4-inch-long stinger, sitting on a tree trunk. My kids and I had come across one here and there over the years, and that stinger had always sent shivers down our spines. This time, as we sat and watched it, we realized that the long stinger wasn't a stinger at all: that bug was laying eggs with it. Then one day while reading *Organic Gardening* magazine, I saw a picture of the insect. It was an adult parasitic wasp. Even though it looked menacing, this was actually a friendly bug that would never hurt me and would certainly help the garden.

It was another epiphany for me, and it reinforced my new-found "organic" thinking. Instead of assuming that every insect was bad, I needed to learn the difference between what was helping my garden and what was hurting it.

During those pre-Internet days, gardening information came from books and magazines. I pored over many glossy color photos, recognizing some of the insects from my own garden. I read about ants farming aphids for their sweet honeydew and learned the difference between striped and spotted cucumber beetles. But more importantly, I was drawn into the garden on hands and knees to witness nature's wonderful balancing act. And ironically, what I learned there was something I should have known all along: a garden can not only survive without chemicals, it can *thrive*.

Doug

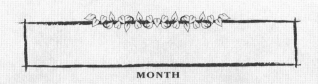

MONTH

PLANT SWAPS

A nice way to make new gardening friends (and obtain some new plant material) is to host a plant swap. Invite every gardener you know, from novice to expert, and ask them to each bring 5 labeled plants. They can be divisions from their own gardens or seeds they have started indoors. Everyone leaves with the same number of plants they brought plus a few new gardening pals.

Of Birds and Corn

If marauding birds steal your corn or pea seeds even before they can germinate, build a maze of jute twine over the area as soon as it's planted. Simply randomly insert several 6-inch branches into the soil and wrap the twine around them, creating a grid of twine about 2 inches above the soil surface. The birds won't risk getting tangled and at the end of the season the string can just go onto the compost pile.

PLEASE EAT
THE FLOWERS

For a beautiful salad,
grow a few edible
flowers to toss with the
spring mix. Marigolds,
nasturtiums, pansies,
roses, borage and many
other garden flowers
make tasty additions
to the plate.

HUMMINGBIRD ATTRACTION

To bring hummingbirds to the garden, plant lots of tubular flowers. Red is a favorite attractant, but the birds drink from most-any-colored trumpet shaped bloom. Hang a sugar water feeder near the garden to lure them in and be sure any water feature has some perching rocks in the shallow parts. Hummers love fine water sprays and mists. It's not unusual to find them swooping in the spray of a sprinkler on a summer morning or preening in the rain.

A WINTER CANVAS

To keep the garden interesting during the dormant winter months, be sure to plant a few attractive small trees. Varieties with persistent fruit (crabapple, hawthorn and Japanese dogwood) or trees with peeling bark (birch, stewartia and paperbark maple) give the winter landscape a much needed boost.

KEEP SUMMER GOING STRONG

If you haven't the heart to
toss out specialty annuals at
season's end, take cuttings
to grow indoors during
the winter months. Many
common container plants
– like sweet potato vine,
lantana, heliotrope, coleus,
silver falls and Persian shield
– are easy to root. Simply
remove a 2-inch-long stem
portion, dip the bottom in
rooting hormone and insert
the cutting into a container
of fresh potting mix. Cover
the pot with a plastic baggie
until roots have formed
(about 1 month) then treat
it like a houseplant until
the spring thaw.

Compost 101

The easiest way to get rich, friable soil is to mix in plenty of compost. It's the not-so-secret ingredient that gives gardeners their green thumb. Compost provides nutrients to your plants, holds water like a sponge and helps prevent disease. It's alive with beneficial microbes that boost the health of both your soil and plants. And, thankfully, compost is something that you can create on your own with just a little effort. By building a compost pile, you'll not only reduce what's taken out to the curb each week, you'll be making an invaluable soil amendment.

Anything that once was living will eventually turn into compost; it's the result of insects, bacteria, fungus and earthworms devouring and processing the materials we add to our pile. If you want to make your own compost, follow these simple instructions.

Our favorite system relies on three bins, each measuring 3'x3'x3' and placed in a row. The bins can be made from used pallets nailed together, concrete block, recycled lumber or even hay bales. We each use this three-bin system, but in a different way. Both of our techniques work great – which one you choose will depend on what kind of effort you want to put forth, how quickly you want to produce compost, and which style suits you best.

In Jess' system, bin number one is the working pile. Into it goes the fresh material (we'll talk about what that is below). As bin number one fills and begins to age, turn the pile by transferring it into the second bin. Each time a bin is filled, its partially decomposed contents are just moved down the line. By the time the material is ready to move out of the third bin, it is finished and ready to spread.

Doug considers his system to be the lazy man's version of composting. Here's how it works: bin number one is filled and then left to rot. Period.

While that bin is cooking, he fills the second bin to capacity and then moves on to start filling the third. Depending on how much composting material you have, the first bin is usually finished and ready to use long before you completely fill the third bin. It takes longer to get the resulting compost, but it's less time consuming to create it. Once the system is set up and the first bin is rotted, compost is always available.

If you don't have the space for a three-bin system, there is also a wide variety of commercial bins and compost tumblers on the market. Because turning your compost can make it decompose up to 50 percent faster (it introduces much-needed air to the microbes), be sure to have your bin located somewhere that is easily accessible.

The perfect compost pile has a 30:1 carbon to nitrogen element ratio, which is created by using three times more carbons than nitrogens – a 3:1 *ingredient* ratio. This means that you'll want roughly three times more dried, brown ingredients (carbon sources) than fresh, green material (nitrogen sources). This will keep your pile's moisture content just right and keep it decomposing at a good clip. This ratio will also keep the pile's temperature around 160 degrees – perfect for rapid decomposition and the safe breakdown of any pathogens present. Green materials include grass clippings, kitchen scraps (no meat, oils or dairy), weeds, fresh trimmings, manure (not from dogs or cats please) and over-ripe veggies. Browns include hay, straw, autumn leaves, shredded newspaper, unbleached napkins and paper towels. Keep a few bags of leaves or a bale of hay right next to the pile, so as summer progresses and you have ample green materials, you can just throw in a few buckets of brown ingredients as you go.

There two more ingredients needed to keep that pile cooking: moisture and oxygen. The oxygen is provided every time you turn your pile. You can also sink a perforated PVC pipe into the pile to get air to the lower layers. As for the moisture, form a slight depression in the top of the pile to collect rainwater. If you're using a closed bin, rinse the kitchen scrap bucket and add the water to the bin. Of course you can also add water from the hose. The ideal moisture content should make your working pile feel like a wrung-out sponge.

Of course, you can always buy bagged or bulk compost at your local nursery, but then you never know what you are getting. You might be spreading bio-solids or you might have just paid a pretty penny for a bag of pine bark nuggets labeled as compost.

Making your own compost is a great way to recycle yard debris and create your own perfect fertilizer. There's nothing better for your plants, and they will love you for giving them everything they need to grow strong.

Vegetable Seed Planting Guide

EARLY SPRING PLANTING*	DAYS TO SPROUTING	DAYS TO HARVEST	DAYS UNTIL PLANTED OUT
Broccoli	5-8	55-65	3-6 weeks
Brussels sprouts	5-8	80-90	3-6 weeks
Cabbage	4-7	60-70	3-6 weeks
Carrots	6-9	65-75	direct sow
Radishes	4-7	25-35	direct sow
Spinach	5-8	45-55	direct sow
Swiss chard	5-8	50-60	direct sow

Plant this group three to four weeks before the last frost.

MID-SPRING PLANTING**	DAYS TO SPROUTING	DAYS TO HARVEST	DAYS UNTIL PLANTED OUT
Beets	5-8	55-65	2-4 weeks
Cauliflower	5-8	50-60	2-4 weeks
Head lettuce	3-6	65-75	2-4 weeks
Leaf lettuce	3-6	45-55	2-4 weeks
Peas	6-9	50-60	direct sow

**Plant this group one to two weeks before the last frost.*

TENDER***	DAYS TO SPROUTING	DAYS TO HARVEST	DAYS UNTIL PLANTED OUT
Beans	7-10	50-60	direct sow
Corn	4-7	65-75	direct sow
Cucumbers	3-6	55-65	direct sow
Squash	3-6	50-60	direct sow
Tomatoes	6-9	55-65	3-6 weeks
Peppers	8-11	55-65	4-8 weeks

***Don't rush this group; wait until danger of frost has passed.*

Your Garden Grid

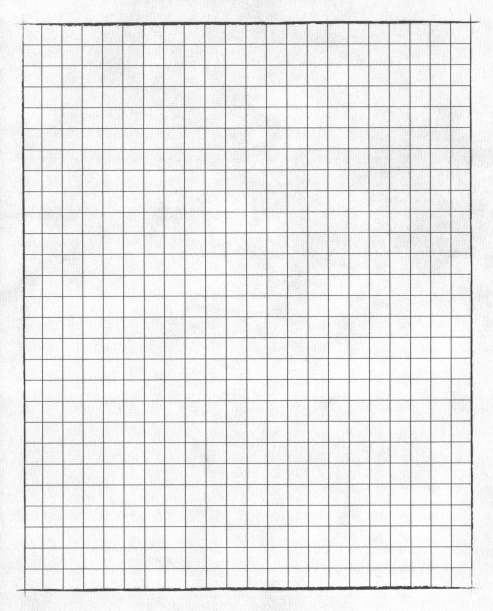

One Square = _____

Your Garden Grid

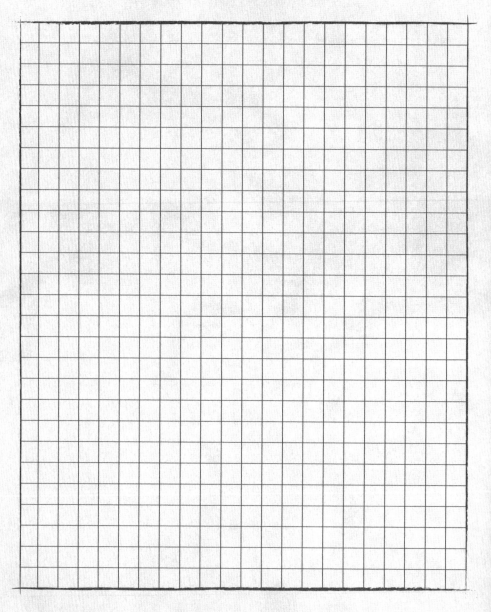

One Square = _____

ABOUT THE AUTHORS

Doug Oster is a garden columnist for the *Pittsburgh Post-Gazette*; his herb and cooking column is distributed nationally by the LA Times Syndicate. He is a regular guest on two Pittsburgh television stations and is a popular lecturer at garden clubs and conferences. Doug is also the author of *Tomatoes Garlic Basil: The Simple Pleasures of Growing and Cooking Your Garden's Most Versatile Veggies* (St. Lynn's Press).

Jessica Walliser has a degree in horticulture. She writes a regular garden column, "The Good Earth", for the *Pittsburgh Tribune Review*, is a frequent contributor to many national and regional gardening publications and lectures at garden clubs and botanic gardens across the country. Jessica is also the author of *Good Bug Bad Bug: Who's Who, What They Do, and How to Manage Them Organically* (St. Lynn's Press).

Doug and Jessica host "The Organic Gardeners" show Sunday mornings on KDKA radio, Pittsburgh. They are the co-authors of *Grow Organic: Over 250 Tips and Ideas for Growing Flowers, Veggies, Lawns and More* (St. Lynn's Press).

They can be reached on the web at:
www.theorganicgardeners.com

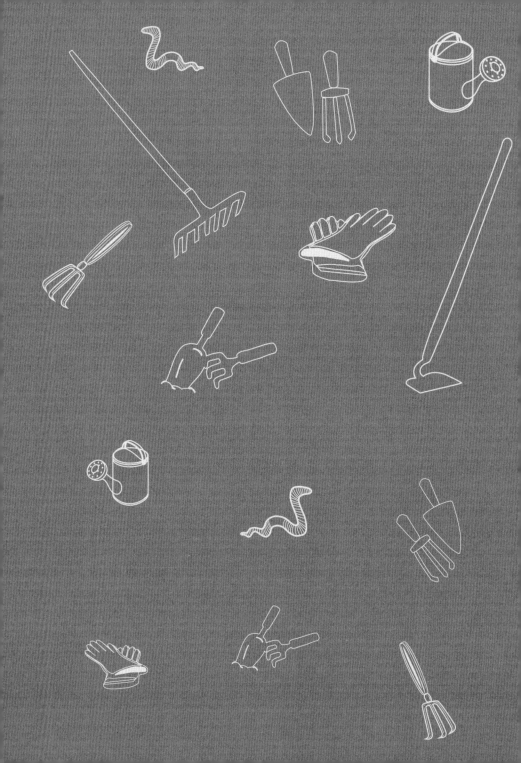